What to do when your mom or dad says . . .
"GET GOOD GRADES!"

By

JOY WILT BERRY

Living Skills Press
Fallbrook, California

Distributed by:

Word, Incorporated
4800 W. Waco Drive
Waco, TX 76710

Dear Parents,

"GET GOOD GRADES!" Do you remember how you felt when your parents said this to you? If you are like most people, your remembrance of the occasion is not a positive one. "Tests" and "grades" . . . both of these are words that evoke a certain kind of negative response from so many of us. The question is why? They are only words that represent inanimate things . . . things that are neither good nor bad in and of themselves, things that have no real power or control. Why, then, do so many of us cringe at the mere mention of these words?

Could it be that tests and grades, while originally intended to be educational aids, have become disciplinary tools to be used to get the student to "shape up" or "toe the line"? The answer to this question may be found in well worn threats such as: "If you don't pass the test, you'll be grounded!" or "If you don't get good grades, you're going to be in trouble!"

The misuse of tests and grades only intensifies the problems parents and educators face in educating children. It only feeds the tension and stress that is so counterproductive to the educational process.

Unfortunately, some adults overreact to this situation by "throwing the baby out with the dirty bath water." They do away with tests and grades altogether, thinking that this will alleviate the problem when in reality it only puts the educator and student at a disadvantage.

What can be done about all of this? If tests and grades are to help instead of hurt, several things need to happen. Parents, educators and students must:

1. Redefine the purpose of tests and grades, making sure that they are seen as educational instead of disciplinary aids.

2. Do away with present notions regarding tests and grades and commit themselves to the accurate definitions.

3. Develop educational programs in which students are personally involved in using tests and grades to further their own education.

4. Equip the students with practical skills that will enable them to get the most out of tests and grades.

This book can help bring these four things about. If you use it systematically (as a part of a continuing program) or as a resource (to be used whenever the need for it arises), you and your child will experience some very positive results.

With your help, your child can and will begin to assume responsibility for his or her own education so that one day you will not have to say: "GET GOOD GRADES" at all.

Sincerely,

Joy Wilt Berry

Has your mother or father ever told you to ...

GET GOOD GRADES!

Whenever you are told to get good grades do you wonder ...

If any of this sounds familiar to you, you're going to **love** this book!

Because it will explain why grades exist, and how you can use them to benefit you.

It's important that you don't waste time going over things you already know, because there's so much for you to learn.

It's also important that you don't skip over things you need or want to know.

To make sure that you don't waste time going over something you already know, or skip over something you need or want to know, you and your teacher must be aware of what you have learned, and what you haven't learned.

The best way to find out what a person has or hasn't learned about a subject is to ask the person questions about it.

Asking a person questions about a subject to find out whether or not he or she knows about it is giving the person a **TEST.**

There are **two kinds of tests.** The first kind is a **verbal** or **oral test**, where the answers to the questions are spoken.

The second kind of test is a **written test**,
where the answers to the questions are written.

But whether a test is oral or written, its main purpose is to find out what you do and do not know.

If the test shows that you know the subject, you can move on to something else.

But if you find out from the test that you don't know the subject, you may want to go back and learn it.

When you give a wrong answer to a question on a test, you are finding out what you don't know.

You are not finding out that you are:
    bad,
    dumb,
    stupid,
    lazy, or
    not as good as someone who answered more of the questions correctly.

Some children who answer questions incorrectly on a test tend to think they are bad, dumb, stupid, lazy, or not as good as someone else, because they think that to be good and acceptable, they must know everything.

These children don't realize that no one person knows everything.

It's impossible to know everything! Even very old, very wise people don't know everything.
Like everyone else, they are constantly learning new things.

If you found the smartest men and women in the world and gave them tests on subjects they knew nothing about, their answers to the test questions would probably be wrong. But that wouldn't mean they were bad, stupid, dumb, or lazy. It would only mean that they didn't know those subjects.

Because a test is a way of finding out what you do and don't know, you should not study just because you're going to take a test.

In other words, you shouldn't learn something just so that you can give right answers to some questions on a test.

Instead, you should learn a subject because it's something you need or want to learn. If you truly learn something, you will automatically be able to answer any questions about it correctly.

Tests help you to know where you stand by showing what you do and don't know.

EVALUATIONS can also let you know where you stand. They can tell you how well you're learning the things you are expected to learn.

There are **two kinds of evaluations**. The first kind is a **verbal evaluation**, in which another person tells you how well he or she thinks you are doing. Student-teacher conferences and parent-teacher conferences are verbal evaluations.

A second kind of evaluation is a **written evaluation**, in which another person writes how well he or she thinks you are doing.

A note or letter written by your teacher is often a written evaluation.

Grades (sometimes called marks) are also a kind of written evaluation. Grades are numbers or letters which show how well a student has learned what he or she is expected to learn.

What does it mean to get a high grade? Does it mean that you are:

> better,
> smarter, or
> more acceptable

than a person who got a lower grade than you did? Absolutely not!

If you get a high grade, it's because you learned a subject and you probably know it well. A high grade means this and nothing more.

There are many kinds of grades. Here are just a few.

One kind of letter grade	What the grade means
A	excellent
B	very good
C	good
D	poor
F	fail
A second kind of letter grade	
E	excellent
S	satisfactory
N	needs improvement
U	unsatisfactory
One kind of number grade	
1	excellent
2	very good
3	good
4	average
5	poor
6	fail

A plus sign beside a letter or number grade means that the student's work is between that grade and the next highest one. For example, a B+ means between A and B. A minus sign beside a letter or number grade means that the student's work is between this grade and the next lowest one. For example, a B- means between C and B. The plus or minus is placed to indicate the grade level which the student's work is closest to. Thus a B- is slightly higher than a C+.

What does it mean when you get a low grade? Does it mean you are:

bad,
dumb / stupid,
lazy, or
not as good as someone who got a higher grade?

Remember, a grade is only an evaluation of whether or not you learned something you were expected to learn.

If you did not learn what you were expected to learn, there's probably a very good reason why.

If you didn't learn something which you were expected to learn, it could have been because **you had problems** that made it impossible for you to concentrate on your schoolwork.

Or you may not have learned something that you were expected to learn because **you weren't ready to learn it**. The subject may have been too difficult for you to understand.

If you didn't learn something that you were expected to learn, it may have been because **you didn't care** whether or not you learned it. Maybe you weren't interested in the subject, or maybe you weren't convinced it was something that you needed to learn.

Or maybe you haven't learned something because **the subject was not presented properly**. It wasn't taught in a way that you could understand or in a way that made you want to learn it.

If you get a low grade, there's always a reason; thus it's very important that you, your parents, and your teacher do two things:

1. Find out what the reason is.
2. Do something about it.

If you can find out why you haven't learned what you were expected to learn, there are many good things you can do next.

If you find out that you haven't been able to learn because of personal problems ...

you may need to spend a great deal of your time and energy dealing with your problems so they won't continue to bother you. Once they are resolved, you can return to your schoolwork. If you are like most children, you may discover that schoolwork will be a lot easier for you when your problems are not getting in the way.

And remember, you will probably need to make sure you have a caring adult helping you as you work on your problems, someone like a parent, teacher, or counselor.

If you find out that you haven't been able to learn because **you weren't ready or the subject was too difficult ...**

there are several things you can do:

1. Talk to your teacher and ask him or her to explain things to you until you understand them. If this doesn't work ...

2. Get someone else to work with you until you understand the subject. The person can be a friend, relative, or tutor. If this doesn't work ...

3. Talk to your teacher and ask him or her to allow you to not work on this subject for a while, until you are ready to try again. You may want to wait for a week, a month, or several months. Your teacher can help you decide how long you should wait to begin working on the subject again.

And remember, it is best if your parents support you and help you with each of these things.

If you find out that you haven't been able to learn because **you're not interested** in the subject or **you're not convinced** that you need to learn
it ...

there are several things you can do:

1. Talk to your parents. Ask them to tell you why it's important to learn about this subject. If they don't know, or if you aren't satisfied with their answer ...

2. Talk to your teacher. Ask him or her to tell you why it's important to learn about this subject. If he or she doesn't give you a good answer, or if he or she says something like, "I don't know, I just teach what I'm told to teach" ...

3. Talk to your principal or the person in your school district who is in charge of the curriculum (the sum of the courses of study in your school).

Getting just one point of view on a subject may not be enough. You may need to get several opinions before you find your questions are completely answered.

Talking to your parents, teacher, principal, and district curriculum director may help you to see the importance of studying a particular subject, and this may make you want to learn it. But even if it doesn't, talking to the adults may make them think again about the necessity of having children learn the subject. It's possible that you may influence them to make a needed change in the curriculum.

Of course, you may end up totally dissatisfied with their answers, and you may never understand why you need to study the subject. If this happens, you will just have to do the best you can.

If you find out that you have not been able to learn because the **subject matter was not presented properly** or taught in a way that made you want to learn, there are several things you can do.

1. Talk to your teacher about it. Kindly tell him or her how you feel and offer suggestions about what could be done to make things more interesting. You may even offer to help the teacher do something unique and exciting. If this doesn't work ...

2. Try to study the subject outside of school. Get your parents, friends, relatives, or other people such as a librarian to help you. Together you may be able to study the subject in a whole new and exciting way.

It's very important for you to know that many children blame everyone but themselves for their problems. Often they blame their teacher for not being interesting or exciting when actually the children are not willing to do what they must do to learn a subject. No one can learn something for you. You must learn it yourself!

So before you blame your teacher or anyone else when you don't learn something, be sure you're being honest and fair. Remember to ask yourself,

> "Am I doing everything I can to learn what I am expected to learn?"

THE END of anxiety and frustration over getting good grades!